Boss Character

By Ashley Marie Knight

Boss Character

Boss Character

Tips and Tools Shared by Self-Made Millionaires

By Ashley Marie Knight

Co-authored by: Lila Holley, Larisha Perlote, Brandy Davidson, Taunya Ford, Charmella Daniels, and Felisha Gibson

Foreword By: Tiffany Rachann

COPYRIGHT ACKNOWLEDGEMENTS

Biblical References:
Scripture quotations marked:
KJV is taken from the King James Bible, Copyright ©1990 by Thomas Nelson Publishing. All rights reserved.

ESV Study Bible. 2008. Wheaton, IL: Crossway Books

Hello reader!

We are so excited you picked up this book. We want to first say congratulations on taking the steps necessary to take yourself and your business to the next level. This book is intended to be your guide on your entrepreneurial journey as you aspire to reach your goals and build your Boss Character.

The book is broken out into chapters written by coauthors who share their stories of their entrepreneurial journeys. These stories are sure to inspire you and motivate you on your toughest days personally and professionally. The Breakout sections are meant to serve as a workbook with prompts to help you assess your strengths and weaknesses. Many of the prompts will push you and make you dig deep. Be honest with yourself because that is the only way you will grow and further develop the Boss Character needed for your next level of success.

Again, thank you for purchasing this book! We look forward to seeing you at the top!

Ashley Marie & the coauthors of *Boss Character*

TABLE OF CONTENT

Be Inspired

FOREWORD

"BOSS". A WORD OFTEN SYNONYMOUS with the interrelatedness of order, acumen, and leadership has been transposed throughout the years. Presently summed as someone who means business, the etymology dates back to the 19th century and translates as *master*–a historical noun for "a man who has people working for him, especially servants or slaves." When considering the historical connotation and how the word has evolved, one can't help but cite the evolution as a continual opportunity to reimagine leadership and all that comes with it conceptually, contextually, and factually. In theory and practice, being a *"BOSS"* isn't a trendy buzzword to be tossed around, promoting the latest and supposed greatest programming regime with empty promises of transformation. Instead, it is to be considered the beginning of infinity, where an emphasis on human capital development and transformation begets positive change. A boss is one that inspires and nurtures BOSS CHARACTER traits and skills in all. Simply put, a real *"BOSS"* understands who they are. Real **BOSS CHARACTER** encompasses the competency and capacity for leading oneself and others, as well as key strategies to sustain goals and objectives, the ultimate being an improved quality of life.

When asked to prepare this foreword, a rarity occurred; I was speechless. As a *"BOSS"*, I was reminded of my commitment to sustain a global educational ecosystem that expands the literacy development standard for communities everywhere. As a sister, it reminded me of my responsibility to share what I have learned from the brilliant **BOSSES** who continue to nurture and support each other beyond. Throughout these pages, you will meet said **BOSSES**. Each of them is a beacon of enlightenment informed by their personal story of trial and triumph for the sake of lasting progress. These women represent what it means to be in a community with those who genuinely look to uphold sacred sisterhood while championing personal and collective economy.

As you reflect on the following pages, I encourage you to nurture and reimagine the **BOSS CHARACTER** in you. I encourage you to consider what order, acumen, and leadership mean, and how they appear in your life.

Lastly, I encourage you to convene with those closest to you, inviting them to do so as well. It's how real change happens, one **BOSS** move at a time.

Tiffany Rachann

Head Imaginarian of @Imagiread

CommuniTEA Educator @Rachannis

Be a BOSS

Breakout Question

What does the word BOSS mean to you?

What does the word BOSS mean to you?

~Brandy Davidson~ I think of two meanings and that is someone that is the *"BOMBDOTCOM"* in one's career, finances, family life, spiritual life, and health-giving positive conquering the world vibes. I also think about how being a *"BOSS"* or someone we may have referred to as a supervisor, is a person in charge of other humans. This role reflects your leadership skills.

~Taunya Ford~ To me, the word "BOSS" signifies being a *Bold Visionary* and an *Outstandingly Resilient Individual* who cultivates supportive sisterhoods and embodies strategic leadership. It represents the strength and vision to lead, the resilience to overcome challenges, the power of unity, and the intelligence to navigate complex situations.

~Ashley Marie~ The word BOSS means to me–to be in a position of influence. The highest position of delegation for any given person or group.

~Felisha Gibson~ It's a person who leads from the front willing to go the extra mile to do what it takes to accomplish the task at hand. They are willing to take accountability for the actions of the team. Give credit when credit is due.

~Charmella Daniels~ To be a boss, especially as a black woman who faced many struggles with self-assurance, self-doubt, and self-image is to embody resilience, strength, and determination. It simply means embracing challenges as opportunities for growth. I refuse to be defined by setbacks and I persistently strive for excellence. Overcoming these obstacles enables me to not only succeed personally and professionally but also inspire others by example through triumph over adversity.

~Lila Holley~ The word BOSS to me is a personality characteristic of someone who, despite all the odds against them, is willing to do what it takes to succeed with integrity and selflessness. A BOSS stands on doing what is right and is willing to take others with them on the success journey.

What do you feel is required to be a BOSS?

_____

_____

_____

_____

_____

_____

_____

_____

_____

_____

_____

_____

_____

_____

What do you feel is required to be a BOSS?

~Brandy Davidson~ I feel that it requires honesty and integrity to be a *"BOSS"*.

~Ashley Marie~ To be a BOSS I believe it requires one to be all in to impact something or someone in any given capacity. I believe it requires one to be personally and professionally sound enough to make a change for the betterment of others. BOSSES render results from their efforts for the good of the cause or the individual that they influence.

~Felisha Gibson~ A BOSS guides and leads the team. A BOSS is willing to listen to the ideas of the team instead of saying their way is the only way. A BOSS provides knowledge, experience, and compassion.

~Charmella Daniels~ Being a Boss requires the representation of empowerment, breaking barriers, and paving the way for future generations.

~Lila Holley~ Attitude is definitely required to be a BOSS. Not a bad or nasty attitude, but an attitude full of determination and grit. This attitude belongs to those who know they are going to go the long haul, work hard, and learn the lessons needed to succeed. Oftentimes others won't understand your drive or passion, but you have to have a focused attitude to not let that bother you to be a successful BOSS.

How we got here…

~Ashley Marie~

IT WAS THIS VERY CONVERSATION that forever changed my thinking about how good, content, and successful I was. Here I was stating *"I'm good"*. I have money. I have a car. I have a home. My marriage is good, and my children are well. This thought was immediately interrupted as I heard my advisor state, "Well all that sounds good. So, since you are good can you give your business partner $300,000 right now if she needs it?" Humff?? Well, I am not *that* good…

The lesson I learned here was we must humble ourselves in all seasons of life. True success can feed some. But, how equipped are you to use what you have to feed others or produce so that others can elevate?

|Break out statement|
> *I know you thought this book was going to be about "YOU" being successful. "YOU" must realize that much success in life comes from the elevation you give something else or someone else.*

Martin Luther King ignited the passion for others to stand in confidence to dream of a better way of living amongst diversity. Jesus cultivated hearts exhibiting the ultimate selfless sacrifice for all people. His actions forever opened a direct connection with God to all who choose to believe in Him. He was described as a charismatic and influential leader who united a diverse group of people. His leadership style was characterized by compassion, humility, and a focus on serving others. Mother Teresa, a selfless servant, dedicated to serving the poorest of the poor, was an extraordinary leader who moved a diverse group of people through her compassion, humility, and commitment to humanitarian work. She managed to inspire and unite people from various backgrounds.

There is a saying, 'You are only as strong as your weakest link'… well, I feel that if you focus on working in unity on any given platform, the strengths of everyone will rise up to create the full masterpiece with little effort.

Are you thinking about being a BOSS? Are you struggling physically, mentally, and financially as a BOSS? This book will give you a reality check. *Boss Character* is your accountability partner. You must silence the busy world around you and find out who you are!

It's okay to be alone. There is another saying that states: 'It is often lonely at the top.' The top is the top because it was not made for everyone to stand up there. It may be true that it's lonely at the top, but not if you focus on your *Top Tier Crew*. Your Top Tier Crew is your 'no holding back' crew who are genuinely in your corner and influence you to continue to grow personally and professionally in any capacity that you need. The truth is no one gets anywhere they are going alone; therefore, you will need the assistance of others to take you to the top. Let's get into how embodying "Boss Character" can help you get there. You must be realistic with your strengths and your God-given purpose.

God's word says,
- Proverbs 16:3 (ESV) – Commit your work to the Lord, and your plans will be established.
- Proverbs 16:9 (ESV) – The heart of man plans his way, but the Lord establishes his steps.
- Proverbs 15:22 (ESV) – Without counsel plans fail, but with many advisers they succeed.

Why have you quit time after time? Why have you QUIT on YOU? Read this book and trust that we will help you gain a clear mind that enforces discipline that cannot be swayed or negotiated. Strengthen your mind and body. Get uncomfortable and make room for a consistent life of success and an overload of blessings!

Breakout Session

What bad habits are keeping you stuck?

_____

_____

_____

_____

_____

_____

_____

_____

_____

_____

_____

_____

_____

_____

Let's Get Started

"Who are you?" Let's map out your identity:

_____

_____

_____

_____

_____

_____

_____

_____

_____

_____

_____

_____

_____

_____

How do you see yourself? How do others see you?

_____

_____

_____

_____

_____

_____

_____

_____

_____

_____

_____

_____

_____

_____

What do you do or aspire to do?

_____

_____

_____

_____

_____

_____

_____

_____

_____

_____

_____

_____

_____

_____

What is the end result when you get there?

_____

_____

_____

_____

_____

_____

_____

_____

_____

_____

_____

_____

_____

_____

There is Power in Positive Words

Describe yourself with 25 positive words here before moving forward.

_____

_____

_____

_____

_____

_____

_____

_____

_____

_____

_____

_____

Blessed are the meek, for they shall inherit the earth ~Matthew 5:5 KJV

Meekness = Power under control

Chapter 1

New Beginnings

~ Ashley Marie~

I STARTED MY FIRST BUSINESS straight out of the military. I saw a problem and I came out into the civilian world determined to solve that problem. As a single mother and leader in the military, my days were sometimes long. I had to report to work for a 5 am meeting, and before that drop off my children at daycare at 4 am, while not leaving work until around 8 pm. This was a stressful experience as a service member. Building a daycare was my heart's joy and the service I provided gave me purpose.

I learned so many lessons in that business. One lesson was using a registration service called Legal Zoom to start that venture. I learned what to do and not to do when filing my business paperwork with that company. In the daycare business, the money comes easy. Working families require childcare and it is a necessity that is essential in today's economy. After three years in this business, life threw me a curveball and I was no longer in business. Even the most prepared business individuals experience losses.

So here I was crushed that my in-home daycare business was no longer operational or provided an income to me. So, in my mind, I had no idea that there was a possibility to earn multiple streams of income at one time. I had been groomed growing up that the process was:

Step 1. Graduate high school.
Step 2. Go to college or the military.
Step 3. Operate in your career field.

Who said that there couldn't be multiple things producing an income for you at the same time? Over the years, after my daycare business closed, I tried so many different things trying to make ends meet and get back on my feet. I tried being a UBER driver, became a nanny, became a bestselling author, volunteered with as many non-profits as I could find, became an administrative assistant for an organization, and finally found my passion with a bookstore that will create generational wealth for my family.

None of these journeys came with easy paths. There were so many ups and downs that ended with exhaustion. Most of these things did not produce enough income, while others produced no income at all. I even experienced a failed partnership.

Notice the income-producing section of these examples? There is such a thing as not enough income being produced and no income being produced. For me, the insufficient income-producing area left me feeling like all my efforts gained me no relief. It didn't matter how much I produced or worked, I never seemed to gain any leverage in my finances. I felt like I was going nowhere fast. This position can leave you feeling hopeless, but there is still hope. So, keep reading but remember these principles. If you find yourself in a *going nowhere-fast* position:

*Start where you are
*Do what you can
*Use what you have

Focus on what you can control.

Now for the no-income-producing hardship, this can be devastating when you are in the thick of it. The reality is you still have bills due, and life is still moving whether you have income coming in or not. The key to this position is to just keep moving. In each community, there are so many outreach programs and events happening in an area near you. Do a little research and get into the rooms that you want to be active in once you get beyond this 'no income coming in' state. It has been my experience many times that when I show up God shows out. It was in those very rooms that I showed up empty that God gave me the refuel that I needed to move forward. If you don't have it (fill in the blank. Whatever it is for you) make it to the rooms who are doing it or have it! There you will find your solution. There is always money to be made each day if you diligently seek the opportunities. Also, develop a discipline that looks beyond monetary compensation in some rooms. There have been many rooms that I placed my physical effort in that gave me more monetary compensation in the future for just that time that I gave a helping hand. Those are lasting relationships.

Not everyone who starts with you will finish with you. People change their minds and life makes you switch lanes for many different reasons. BOSSES must stick and stay. You must set it in your mind that this is what I am going to do, or this is what I am not going to do. Saying yes to it and saying no to it are both important BOSS Characteristics to have. You must make sound decisions fast so you do not lose as much when things are not profiting you or happening as you projected they would. My daycare business required me to be in my home from 5am - 8pm, which left no room for self-care and or necessary needs like grocery shopping and paying bills on time. I couldn't make it to doctors' appointments, and I most definitely couldn't enjoy a nice lunch with a friend in that season of my life. When I had to shut down my daycare business, I didn't understand why, but now I understand. You cannot be confined to a box when you are a creative person who needs room to grow and thrive. Stop boxing yourself into one way of living.

Small beginnings we aim to multiply.

~Dr. Ann James

What have your bad habits cost you?

~Amy Morin

Be sound in your decision-making practices.

Chapter 2

Stop Playing

~Brandy Davidson and Ashley Marie~

EMBODY THE STRENGTH THAT once excelled from within you when you don't have the courage to try. Sometimes you have to put on your armor of FAITH and say: "*not today, satan, not today*!" I have the desire to help myself and all of those that I love but the day-to-day trials of life can do a number on your confidence, discipline, health and most of all finances. Taking this journey with these amazing warrior women has been a breath of fresh air for me. Here we are in a divided world operating as one unit together. We set a goal to become millionaires in 12 months and we put the plan into action! I am thankful that I was in the right room at the right time to go on this journey beyond fear. I wanted to close the debt gap in my family and put myself in a wealthy position to change my mindset on how I would walk in my purpose in life. Sometimes those hard lessons teach you a great solution model to bring out others from the same mistakes. My advice to you would be to walk it out beyond how you feel or what you think. Apply the discipline it takes to reach your goals now before it's too late.

There is another way. One of my previous business partners used to always say, "There are more than 10 ways to skin a cat!" I took that statement with me beyond that partnership because it always reminded me that there was always another way to get there. I just have to slow down, process the information, and shorten the direction. You must always be ready to pivot in life. Unfortunately, you can't just have it your way, it is most definitely not Burger King. You can make it happen if you just find other ways.

God never leaves you without a lifeboat in the situations that you find yourself in. Survival 101–you must stay focused and calm. You have to keep your mind clear to process the situations that are placed before you. Most of the recorded miraculous heroism is quoted on the mere fact that fight or flight kicked in and they stepped into action to save someone or something in a moment's glance. We all can survive anything. Failure is never final. Just stay focused on your goal and you will get there.

Let's do this exercise:
Tell yourself, "I can no longer hold myself back."
Write three things that can help you get there using the three prompts below.
Example: I will show up. I can show up. I am confident enough to walk into the room.

I will

_____

_____

_____

_____

I can

_____

_____

_____

_____

I am

_____

_____

_____

_____

_____

Where are you holding yourself captive/back/stagnant? (List that here)

_____

_____

_____

_____

_____

_____

_____

_____

Action will get you there.

~Ashley Stahl

Be confident in your source.

Chapter 3

Show Up

~Charmella Daniels~

Hearing and Adhering to God's Voice

BECOMING A BOSS TAKES AUDACITY, determination, and a keen sense of knowing who you are. Life has a way of testing you to the farthest limits possible. How we choose to respond to life's many hurdles shapes our character as we become older and wiser. For me, the major factor that determined the outcome of my difficult situations, when becoming a boss, has been the ability to not only hear but adhere to God's voice. I often ask myself three questions to help me determine whether I am hearing God's direction.

1. *Was His voice loud and clear when you heard it*?
2. *What spiritual space were you in when He spoke to you*?
3. *Did He send confirmation*?

The adherence comes when I am spiritually connected through prayer, reading, and meditation.

Have you ever heard God's voice? Many people questioned whether or not they hear God's voice. Since I was a young teenage girl, I could hear God's voice. However, I didn't always adhere to His instructions. In every situation when I chose not to listen, it most certainly led to a much less desirable outcome. None of those circumstances or failures have been in vain. As I become more seasoned and experienced, I've learned to not only hear but adhere to the voice that leads me in every area of my life.

Becoming a boss hasn't been an easy road. It has taken nurturing and major lessons learned to arrive at this stage. Serving my country has been one of my most proud accomplishments. It came with fears, tears, and a countless number of struggles. But I have heard God's voice through it all. Whether asking about the next duty assignment location, a good school for my sons, or the right career move, I would always pray to God for guidance. And He would always provide an answer. It wasn't always immediately that He would reply. The funny thing about receiving answers to your request is that they don't always align with what you think the answer should be. I can assure you, however, that the answer you receive is always the right one.

There were many things that I struggled with coming up as a young black girl being raised in rural Mississippi. Things like being painfully shy, feeling unattractive, and lacking self-confidence are issues that presented themselves daily in my life. Those negative thoughts are not conducive to being a boss in any category. God blessed me profoundly with a natural ability to perform (act) and gave me a pretty good singing voice too. From middle school to high school, I competed in countless events as well as performed at various locations in and around my state. My trophy box to this day holds all the great memories of competitions and tournaments in which I displayed my natural talent given to me from above. The thrill of seeing my competitors and knowing that I would crush them gave me confidence that I would carry throughout my life. Although some viewed it as cockiness, it was the total opposite. You see when you understand that you have a divine gift, meaning it came from God, you walk differently, you talk differently, and you show up differently. It took me years to figure out how to tap more into my divine gift than accept the demeaning self-image placed upon me during my early years.

I absolutely enjoyed performing on stage and in front of an audience. When playing a character or performing a poetry piece, every negative thing in my life, if only for a moment, would disappear. As I embodied these characters and experienced an altered reality, I realized that the confidence I showed during the performances was my true character. And the personality that I showed off stage was a mere illusion of who I was created to be. I was born with boss attributes and needed to find a way to display them whether on or off stage, which I would eventually do.

Becoming an actress had to be my calling, or so I thought. One of my early encounters with hearing God's voice was, Him revealing to me that I would travel the world and meet lots of new and exciting people. He also confirmed that I would be in front of audiences and continue doing the things that I loved with passion. His voice was loud and clear. I couldn't be happier that He saw fit to bless me with the desires of my heart. Later I would find out that if your spiritual position is off, you can easily misinterpret the message. My spiritual position when I heard this message was a bit tainted as I was engulfed in the wild world of teenagersim.

By the time I reached 17 in high school, my then-boyfriend (now husband) and I had our first son. My family, teachers, and community all came together to support me in various ways because they too saw something special in me and told me so, regularly. During Christmas 1994, a very pregnant teenage girl (me) was told by two inspirational teachers (Ms. Clanton and Mr. Williams) that "you will participate in all events." Embarrassed by the stigma that comes with being a teenage mother, I found it difficult to be on stage and in front of an audience. I cried and asked repeatedly to not have to participate. After receiving a firm, no, I decided to boss up! In my opinion, I was the best-performing pregnant teenager to grace the stage of my alma mater. God will always place people in your life who will help elevate you to the next level no matter your circumstance. These two teachers did just that for me. I performed pregnant, got good grades, and advanced to a senior in high school.

Fast forward to my senior year, I worked very hard to be the best drama student on the team. Additionally, I mentored all the young aspiring students to go hard for their goals. It was simple, God gave me talents, He surrounded me with supportive people, and all I had to do was hone my craft so that when the opportunity came, I would be ready. Following my drama teacher's advice, I entered every possible competition and almost always won either first or second place (an early display of my boss character). My final act as a senior was playing Co-Co from the hit series "Fame" and it would be my last grandstand before I set off to become the greatest actress in theater or on the movie screen. But as life would have it, it wasn't my last opportunity to act. Turns out, I was selected to compete in the finals for a state drama competition. This extraordinary event could change the trajectory of my acting career. The problem was my graduation ceremony, and the competition were happening on the same day. I could not do both. The opportunities that could follow, if I won, were endless. I prayed about it. Everything I received from that prayer said to go to the competition to secure my future goals. After all, I was already done with high school and the ceremony was only a celebration of that accomplishment. Was this the big break I had waited for? Why did I have to choose?

On graduation night, my family cheered loudly as I walked across the stage to receive my diploma. This was the first time both my mom & dad attended one of my events at the same time even though I had been performing for over four years. The night was very special, but I couldn't help thinking about what I would be doing had I chosen to participate in the competition. I don't remember much else from that weekend. And the decision to not adhere to His voice has left me wondering for years, what if….

Shortly after graduation, I vowed to never make that same mistake again. Over the next few years, regret would overcome me. I worked pointless jobs and wasted precious years of my life. With no money to travel for casting calls, being a teenage mother, and having nothing but my past accomplishments to show for, self-destruction seemed inevitable. Again, I found myself becoming that little girl who was shy, unattractive, and unsure of herself. I would never know the opportunities that could have presented themselves. I would never know if those scholarships would have my name on them had I gone. I would never know if I could have beaten the young lady who I had battled all year long. I later found out that she won first place and often wondered how her life turned out.

The life God had shown me was starting to look impossible to achieve. I tried many things like junior college, looking for local acting opportunities, and even moving out of state; however, nothing seemed to be happening for my career. Feeling frustrated, defeated, and assuming I had heard the wrong message, I turned back to God for clarity. This time, I was given instructions to go to the military. The military is something I had never considered before, because how can I be on Broadway and serve my country at the same time? Although I heard God's voice telling me to go to the military, I did not adhere, initially. The contradiction with my self-appointed destiny kept me in limbo for some time. It seemed as though everything around me began to confirm what I had already been told. The famous

"Be All That You Can Be" commercial seemed to come on every time I walked into a room. When talking to random people, we would end up discussing the military in some way. I eventually started having multiple dreams about the military. After various signs of confirmation, I decided to go speak to a recruiter.

The year is now 1997 and it almost broke me. I found myself with child again. I gave birth to our second son at 19 years old. I experienced postpartum depression for several months because the feeling of failure had become so heavy I couldn't pull myself out of it. To add to my already failing life, my father passed away a few months after my second child was born. He met his grandson and got to hold him before he left this world. Our relationship was headed towards a positive path, and I wished I had more time with him. Had he stayed around a few more months, he would have been able to be there for my wedding. His absence left me feeling angry & abandoned. The military seemed like a great way to escape the havoc that started overtaking my life. The little girl I had fought so hard to suppress was back and running my entire life.

When my husband first asked for my hand in marriage, it was an immediate yes! This was something I had dreamt of, had visions of, and prayed for. Isn't it every girl's desire to have a beautiful family, raise your children with the person you love, and live happily ever after? Or was that only in the fairy tale books I'd read? At the age of twenty, what could I possibly know about marriage? The news wasn't received very well on either side, so I began to doubt my decision. My heart never changed but my mind got the best of me and soon doubt, fear, and uncertainty set in. This appeared to be the normal routine of things after I chose to adhere to God's word.

As with almost everything in my life up to this point, I sought God's counsel regarding marriage. Although He had already made it clear to me that it was always my husband, for some reason I still needed "reconfirmation". It's important to note that I'd ask God for patience with me as well, on the regular. I referenced those same three questions. Was His voice loud & clear? What spiritual space were you in? And did He send confirmation? Taking into consideration that I was a single mother of two sons, still living at home, with no formal education & no real plan for my future life, it was hard to answer the second question. However, when my life is in shambles and my mental stability is off, I fiercely seek God in a way that is different than when life is going well for me. To answer question two, I was in a pretty good spiritual space.

My wedding ceremony was beautiful, and my life appeared to finally reflect my prayers. The man I married was indeed a prayer answered by God. Due to being violated as a young teenage girl, at about fourteen, I began asking God for a man who would always protect me. I asked God to ensure that the man He sent would love me unconditionally and treat me with respect. I also asked God to make sure he would be the father of my sons. This specific request was because I never wanted anyone to mistreat my children just because they weren't biologically theirs. Yes, I prayed for boys and ultimately ended up with three of them. Although our relationship was far from perfect, I knew my husband was sent from above and this was confirmation that God hears me. I must have asked God to send the right man to me over ten times as I got older, and my husband was the only one who appeared each time. It was always him. How then, did the end of my wedding day involve pepper spray, a gun, and police, I wondered. That will be a story for another time. The incident, as bad as it was, motivated me to get certified, qualified, and get the hell out of Mississippi ASAP! I was headed to boot camp three months after my nuptials.

Within seven months, I had given birth, lost my father, turned twenty, got married, and went off to the military leaving behind a newborn, a two-year-old, and a new husband. I cried a lot and wondered often if I had heard God correctly about the military. Was this my true calling? Did adherence require suffering? Does obedience equate to heartbreak? Would God make me an actress after this process was over? These were the questions that I asked myself as I embarked on my new life as a Soldier. I had to refer back to my confirmation questionnaire. And yes, His voice was loud and clear, yes, I was in a good spiritual space and yes, He confirmed it, several times. Doubt and fear have a way of creeping into your mind especially when you are about to follow God's command. Just trust the process.

I gave up on being an actress shortly after entering the military. I was growing up and becoming a woman. Being an actress became a childish thought in my mind. My responsibilities outweighed my personal goals. Had God even really said He would make me an actress anyway? The two little boys that I came home to every day became my motivation in life. Soon, I was no longer depressed and began to love my role as a mother, wife & Soldier. As I evolved, that lost little girl started to fade away. Thank you, Lord. My life was good, and my family was thriving.

Three years was my initial commitment to the military. However, I would go on to serve for over twenty-two years. Quickly climbing the leadership ladder, I found myself on a third deployment because of September 11th's attack on American soil. By this time, I had completed ten years of service. Through my service, I met so many new and interesting people. I loved interacting with people from all walks of life. The bonds built with some of these individuals have lasted for well over twenty years. Traveling became an exciting part of our family's activities. The adventures of seeing new places and experiencing new things to do was a thrill to all of us. My family and I lived overseas for a period and made the most of our time there.

During this deployment, in addition to my normal job, I was assigned the responsibility to be an equal opportunity advocate. The job entailed acknowledgment of ethical holidays and ensuring all people were treated fairly. During deployments, individuals often experience a high level of stress. Being away from family, working extended hours, and having limited access to call home takes its toll after a while. Obviously, I could relate, seeing as though I would be gone from my now three sons & husband for a year as well. A Black History Celebration came to mind in an effort to take individuals' minds off of their current situation and location. My goal was to get everyone involved and I did just that. In a month, I was able to put together a full production. I tapped back into my time as a high school drama student and used everything I learned. With very limited resources and time my team and I successfully arranged a two-hour production that received the highest accolades from seniors, peers, and participants. From the sound guy to the food team, they all thanked me for giving them a small break from their current reality. You see, I used my past experiences as well as the leadership skills taught to me by the military to make an impact on others' lives. As mistress of ceremony, I was commended on my presentation and ability to speak in front of an audience. This would not be the last time as I would do the same for Cinco Demayo and Indian Heritage Month. It all started to make sense. The experiences that I had as a young teenager were preparing me for moments like these.

My military career was filled with exciting experiences, colorful people, and learning experiences that could only have happened while serving my country. Not only did the experience push me to new heights, but my family also benefited as well. The boys flourished at each duty assignment. They were well-rounded, versed, and could fit in any environment they were in. They too were bitten by the "big stage" bug as they performed on many stages both dancing, speaking, and acting. My husband created friendships that will last a lifetime and took much pleasure in watching his family excel on many levels. Oftentimes, I would take a breath and thank God for always directing my path. Understanding that God knows better than me what's good for me is the best life lesson I've learned to date.

By the year 2017, I was nearing the end of my career. I made plans to exit the military after our sons reached a certain age and I had completed at least twenty years of service. I'd always had veterans in my life telling me that I would know when the time was right. After discussing my decision at length with my husband, we decided the time was right. In addition, we both started to work on building our own trucking company. The only thing left to do was to submit a request and wait for retirement approval. I could hardly contain the excitement.

Prior to the request being submitted, I was notified out of the blue that I had been selected to deploy for a fourth time. My initial thought was that there is no way I am going again. My plans had already been made. Plus, I really felt like I had done my part. Three deployments were enough. And although my sons were much older, I didn't want to leave them for another year-long stint. Before the deployment notification, my health was not great. I had been seeing a physician regularly and I discussed with her the notification of the upcoming deployment. She explained to me the effects it could have on my health and told me that if I started treatment, I would not qualify for deployment. It was a lot to take in so I requested that she postpone treatment for a little while longer so that I could weigh my options.

I spoke to my husband immediately and like most other military spouses, he was not happy about the news. He also reminded me of my health status and recommended that I start the treatment as my physician had advised. This would stop me from going. For the next few weeks, I struggled with the situation before me. It was during this time, I heard God's voice telling me to go on this deployment.

Questioning God is not something I try to do, but in this case, I did. Why me, was one of the first questions to come to mind. I also remember asking, "Didn't I do my part already?" I had vivid dreams and realistic visions about the things I would be doing during the deployment. On a daily basis, I found myself going back and forth.

Once again, I found myself going back to those three faithful questions I had referred to many times before in my life, so I asked myself. 1. Was His voice loud and clear? 2. What spiritual space were you in? 3. Did He send confirmation? When I answered these questions, I delivered the news to my husband, my family, and my physician that I had to go. Neither of them could understand why I would go, seeing as though I didn't have to go. Soon after, I began preparing for the journey and my previous plans would be put on hold as I knew I had to adhere to God's voice if I wanted to walk in my purpose and be the boss He created me to be.

Deployment "four" was the most challenging one of all. It was also the one where I grew the most, spiritually. To say I was pushed to the brink would be an understatement. I enjoyed every minute. By the time the deployment was over, I had led a women's ministry group, managed all "gospel service" activities, served as mistress of ceremony for many events and so much more. In this setting, I saw God's plan manifesting itself. Obviously, I was traveling. Some of the individuals I met during this tour are still very close to me. There are five specific women (The Bagram Fav 5) whom I formed a special bond with and we will be connected for life. As for my job during that time, I experienced lots of success. The things I was able to accomplish in one year came as a complete surprise to me. The deployment seemed to have flown by really fast. And when it was time to leave, I had never felt more accomplished. The feeling you get when you listen and obey God's plan is unexplainable. Per usual, He always knows what's best. Now that the deployment was over, I could head back and get prepared for my next chapter of life. Stay tuned.

Previously I told you of how I could hear God's voice from an early age. My grandmother always shared her life's experiences with me. She is the one who talked to me about how much God loves me and how He would direct my path if I asked Him to. I believed her. When God told me that I would travel and meet new people, I believed it. I added my own twist to the message and assumed that it meant by way of acting. Although I wasn't acting, I still was able to perform in various ways. Due to my occupation in the Army, I consistently had an audience to which I spoke whether it was teaching, training, or briefing other Soldiers and sometimes family members. Praise dancing was also added to my resume, which my good friend and mentor Princess helped me to explore. Acting was clearly not in the cards for me. That realization made it easy to fully embrace my true purpose. I don't know how my life would have turned out had I become an actress, but I would be willing to bet, not as good as the one I've already had. Understanding His purpose for me would be a process that I had to constantly tap into, and I wouldn't change a thing about my life's journey.

Knowing it and doing it...are two different things.

~Amy Morin~

Breakout Questions

What is your life's assignment?

_____

_____

_____

_____

_____

_____

_____

_____

_____

_____

_____

_____

_____

Be Loyal

Chapter 4

Building a Legacy

~Lila Holley~

You Want to Be Successful–Get a Team!

If You Want to Go Farther, Get a Team

THE GREATEST GIFT THAT MY 22-year Army career gave me was the experience of being a part of a team. I learned in the Army that success requires a team. To accomplish any mission, I always relied on my team. Every person was important for the success of the mission. Throughout my career and at every stage of my career, I can recall a person/people who was/were instrumental and invested in my professional development, growth, and overall success in the military. So, after my 22-year career ended and I transitioned to the next chapter of my life, I was very thankful for the experience the Army afforded me, specifically the experience of what true, successful teamwork looked like. I remembered this as I stepped into entrepreneurship. My first stop on the path of entrepreneurship following my military career was working in a family business, a restaurant. We were a small staff, and everyone was crucial in making sure all tasks were completed from day to day. I recall one day when we had two back-to-back catering events – a large group meeting of local pastors and a baby shower. We had about 45 minutes between the two events, and it was hectic because if you know anything about pastors…they like to talk! So, we had to politely get them out of the restaurant so we could set up and decorate for the baby shower. As soon as the pastors had cleared the building, I went into Army mode barking out orders. Everyone executing their assigned tasks was critical to our success. We needed the dishwasher to wash the dishes. We needed the cook to prepare the food for both events, breakfast for the pastors, and lunch for the baby shower patrons. The wait staff/hostess team needed to decorate and set up the restaurant for the baby shower.

Everyone did their part, and the day went off without any major hiccups. We ran like a well-oiled machine, like a well-run team. We were proud of what we were able to accomplish just by working together as a team.

Obviously, there are some business models where you must have a team to operate. One person could not run a brick-and-mortar restaurant by themself. They could try, but they would run themself ragged. So, when I became a solopreneur, a one-person business, I kept these experiences in the back of my mind. I mean, I could be an author and speaker and do it all by myself. I saw women doing it every day. Therefore, I repeated the solo practice, I did–I did it all by myself. I booked my speaking engagements, posted my social media posts, wrote my newsletter and blogs, and traveled to events lugging suitcases and boxes full of books. But we know how the saying goes, 'If you want to go fast, go alone. If you want to go far, go together.' It's more than just a mere quote or a nice saying…it's true! I was wearing myself out! I needed help and I needed it fast because the business was growing fast, and it became hard to manage alone. Besides that, there were tasks that I did not enjoy. Oh, I could do the tasks, but it was mentally taxing because I did not enjoy it and I would rather be doing something else. As an entrepreneur, you must do self-assessments along the way to check on and keep track of your mental well-being and your business systems and practices. This is a needed practice and helps you grow your business over time. The person you are when you start or the systems you implement when you begin your business will not be the same as when you grow your business and start making six figures in sales in your business.

After assessing my situation, I knew I needed help, so I set out to get some. First, I prayed and asked God to send me some help, nothing specific at this time– just help. I then made a list of the daily, weekly, and monthly tasks I had to complete as a solopreneur. I ranked them from most enjoyable to least enjoyable. From this list, I was able to be a little more specific in my prayer time, I knew exactly what I needed help with. I then looked at my budget and decided on what I could afford to pay for someone to take over different tasks. I also looked at where I could ask for volunteers or free labor to assist. Just starting as an entrepreneur, money may be tight. Many of us bootstrap our businesses, especially minority or woman-owned businesses as these businesses historically receive the least amount of bank and venture capitalist (VC) funding. I used my own money, savings, and funds from my family to start my business. According to a McKinsey Company report in 2022, women-founded teams received 1.9 percent of VC funds and only 0.1 percent of VC funds went to Black and Latino women founders. [1] These statistics are shameful but reality, and something entrepreneurs need to be aware of before going into business so they can plan accordingly. This is why a mastermind group like Empowered Sisters Network (ESN) and other groups like ours are so important– WE ARE THE BANK.

I digress. Back to building my team…I realized I needed an accountant, a brand manager/social media manager, and a lawyer on my team. These were specialized areas where I realized I did not have the expertise needed to successfully handle these tasks within my business. I worked to find professionals who could work within my budget. Then I sought volunteers within my support network to assist me as I traveled to events. What a relief it was when I finally found the help I needed.

So, how did I do it? Simple–I asked! I know asking for help may be difficult for many. We feel like we have to do it all and have all the answers for everyone else. Newsflash You do not have superpowers! You may be strong and amazing in your own right–but you are not superhuman, and you are not expected to be. At some point we all need help and the beautiful thing I discovered was that when I asked for help or advice, there were so many willing to help, share their knowledge, and share their lessons learned. I asked other entrepreneurs I met on my journey. I started attending conferences, seminars, workshops, and other events geared toward helping women start and run successful businesses. This tactic not only helped me find the team members I needed but it helped me grow my network and support system of other like-minded entrepreneurs. This was the manifestation of the quote, 'If you want to go fast, go alone. If you want to go far, go together.'

---

[1] https://www.mckinsey.com/featured-insights/diversity-and-inclusion/underestimated-start-up-founders-the-untapped-opportunity#/ Dominic-Madori Davis, *"The highs and lows of Q3 venture capital data for women startup founders,"* TechCrunch+, October 14, 2022; Dominic-Madori Davis, "Women-founded startups raised 1.9% of all VC funds in 2022, a drop from 2021," TechCrunch+, January 18, 2022.

As an entrepreneur, you may need to perform all the tasks in your business yourself starting out, but that method is not sustainable, it will wear you out both mentally and physically. I recommend planning for and positioning yourself to build a team of professionals to help you on your journey. Be prepared to allocate these expenses in your budget. The cost may initially be a sacrifice but in the long run, it will be worth it. Having access to a knowledgeable lawyer and accountant is priceless, protects you and your business, and saves you money over time. Building a network of supporters around you who are willing to volunteer their time to help you grow your business is a true blessing. So, ask, the worst they can say is 'no,' but keep asking because your 'yes' may be right around the corner. If you don't ask, you will never receive what it is that you need.

Teamwork Makes the Dream Work

I know this sounds like a corny cliché but it's more than that, and more importantly, it is true. I know firsthand that it takes a team to build a dream. My dream started with a book...one book. That's all I had in my mind. I wanted to write a book because I wanted to help people, more specifically, I wanted to help Veterans. As an entrepreneur, you must get clear on your vision for your business. This includes your 'why', who your ideal customer is, what their main pain point is, and how you will solve this for them or how you will serve them. So even as an author, someone just wanting to share my story, I had to go into it with a business mindset. While the focus was wanting to help people, the overall goal was more than that. I had to build something I could maintain that I would be able to scale/grow, and that would be profitable. I had to go into writing a book like I was starting a business, because I was. I already mentioned how I built my network. On my journey, I connected with an amazing network of badass women entrepreneurs. They had done it all and were willing to share their knowledge, experiences, wins, and lessons learned from their losses. I sat at their feet and soaked in all the wisdom they were pouring out. These women acknowledged me, applauded my dream, and celebrated my vision. They believed in me and my dream, and they believed it could be done. More importantly, they believed I could do it! This was all I needed to take my dream and run with it.

As I learned from this network of intelligent women, I noticed a few things taking place within me. The first thing I recognized was my confidence grew. I went into entrepreneurship not knowing anything about running a business. I was a Veteran. I served 22 years in the Army and had no business degrees and no business management background. But I was a leader, and I had a finisher's mindset because I had completed so many different things in my military career–military schools, deployments, assignments, and a whole 22-year career. My network made me believe I could learn where my knowledge fell short and that I could achieve the goals I had set for myself. The funny thing about confidence is that it makes you believe you can do more and more. And that is exactly what I did–more! But I cannot take full credit for the growth that has taken place over the years, I have to give God all the credit. As I grew in confidence and as I accomplished things on my journey, God grew my vision and purpose. He grew my dream. He fueled my creativity. He placed the right people around me to inspire, motivate, and support me on my journey. God made every opportunity that came my way available to me. People have asked me over the years how I did this or how I came up with that and when I respond that it was all God, I get mixed responses. Some people get it while others are expecting some secret sauce or magic pill. As an entrepreneur, be clear about your motivation. Know what fuels your passion.

For me, it's knowing that God has called me to this work and that He is guiding me on this journey. I know I could not have done any of this without Him. As a result of my confidence growing, my vision of my dream grew as well. As I mentioned, it began with one book. That's all I had in me when I started this journey. But as I shared with the ladies in my network about my dream and my 'why' the more they shared with me how they could see it and how impactful it would be. They gave me ideas and shared examples of what I could do with my dream. I asked God to expand my dream and He did just that. At the time of this writing, I am preparing to publish my 11th book! As an entrepreneur, you must continue to grow yourself, your vision, and your business. Whatever that looks like to you is how you do it. Whether you stay grounded in your faith, seek out coaching, earn a degree, or surround yourself with an amazing supportive network is not important, you could do all these steps (that's what I did). What's most important is that you take steps to continue to grow. If you do this entrepreneur thing right it will come naturally because you won't be satisfied just staying stagnant.

Lastly, I already mentioned this, but I cannot say it enough–ask for help. I'll be honest, this was not easy for me. I was not used to asking for help. In the military, I was trained so I would know how to do my job. Because of my training, I knew what to do to accomplish the mission. I became part of a team, so we were each other's help, and no 'ask' was needed. This amazing network of women that I connected to showed me that there was strength in asking for help and providing help to others. Put your pride to the side and ask! You will be surprised how many are willing to help, to share, to encourage. When I asked my network, I found that with every question I asked and received an answer to, I saved time, energy, stress, and in many instances money. Today I am fortunate to be able to have experienced enough on this journey that now I can offer advice and help to others. I want us all to win. I am always humbled when asked my opinion or advice about something and I am honored to be able to pour into others on this entrepreneur journey.

So, as you can see, 'teamwork makes the dream work' is truly more than a cool quote or motivational slogan to say as you embark on this journey of entrepreneurship. It is the very actions needed on this journey. It is the thing needed to get started, stay the course, and push through the hard days…because they are coming. I am forever indebted to this amazing network of women who believed in me in the beginning and the ones who have joined me on my way. The ones who poured into me when I needed it most because they helped grow my confidence in myself. The ones who provided an example of what success looked like when I began my journey of entrepreneurship. I've never forgotten the lessons they taught me and as a result, have made it part of my journey to give that same energy back to those I have encountered on my way. Teamwork makes the dream work. If you have a dream, make an effort to surround yourself with a team. A team that believes in you because, on those days when the dream ain't working, that team will give you what you need to keep going, to keep pushing.

Teams Hold You Accountable

I remember early on my journey of entrepreneurship, I worked so hard. I mean I was on my grind! I had a lot of energy and I worked hard. Don't get me wrong, I loved it because I was working on my dream. I remember the long days and late nights. I remember traveling and lugging all those heavy books and merchandise with me. The reason I recall this time on my journey is because of the little things. The little things that may seem insignificant to someone else but make a world of difference to you. Little things like realizing that I am a 'sweater'. I sweat easily whenever I do anything physical. I could work out, get dressed, or walk to the corner–I'm going to sweat! Because of this, whenever I traveled and was scheduled to do a book signing, speak, or engage supporters in any way, I had to make sure I had a fresh shirt to wear when it was time to greet the audience and that I wore plenty of deodorant. I also deal with back pain, so I had to make sure I brought my flat shoes with me to events that required me to be on my feet for an extended time. Again, I know these seem like small, useless details but to those chasing the dream of becoming a business owner, small things are important to think about as you prepare for this journey.

I share this part of my journey because for years I did this by myself or with one other person who volunteered to help me out. As I stayed focused on doing the work to build my dream, I was being watched. I was being admired from afar. I didn't know this, but it was a welcomed gift that came in the form of a team, a team of people who wanted to protect me and take care of me. I was extremely humbled because I didn't even know I needed this type of help but when it came, I welcomed it. As I became more comfortable with this extra help, I grew and was able to accomplish even more.

This special type of help came from two women, specifically–Ashley Knight and Brandy Davidson. I have to name them because they did and continue to do so much for me and this beautiful community we've built serving women Veterans. When Ashley traveled with me for the first time, she was amazed at how much I did to execute an event. I packed up the car, I made all the travel arrangements and reservations, I covered all our expenses and I coordinated with the event point of contact. It was a lot but who was going to do it if not me? She then observed me during the event and told me she admired how I gave each supporter my undivided attention and was present in the moment with them–it wasn't only about making the sale; it was about making a genuine connection with the person. I told her I appreciated that she took the time to observe all of that. I remember when I was in their shoes and just wanted to be heard, so I make sure I stop and listen and give that time and focus to anyone sharing their story with me. Ashley helped me manage my events, but she also helped me stay true to my calling in this business. I remember praying for help and being specific, asking for someone who saw my heart for this work, someone who believed in my vision as much as I did–I realize I prayed for Ashley. She would probably tell you that I was a little reluctant at first, and I must admit that I was. I mean this business is my baby, I birthed it, and I wasn't going to just hand it over to just anyone. I needed to know that Ashley would love it as much as I did–and she did! She was the missing link that not only I needed but, this Sisterhood needed, period. She is my eyes and ears where I cannot see or hear, and I appreciate that so much.

Then came along Brandy Davidson. She also provided a type of help that I didn't realize I needed. I like to think of Brandy as a protector. She is here to protect the business/brand and me. She makes sure that I eat and have water to drink. She acts as a buffer and handles things that I don't need to worry about because they will eat up my time from doing something else. Most importantly, she holds me accountable to my vision, mission, and purpose of the business. She has my back even when I think or say, 'I got it.' Whenever Brandy says my name in that calm, melodic voice, I know I need to step aside and let her handle it. I just chuckled and let her take the lead. I can say with confidence that I have no problem letting my teammates lead at times because they are women who have strong leadership skills. Not only are we all women Veterans, but we respect each other's skills and abilities. We are truly better together. What I learned from these women is that a good team, one that truly cares for you and your success, will hold you accountable not only in business things but also regarding your overall well-being. I appreciate it when Brandy makes me slow down and eat before an event or tells me to take a break from texting or emailing regarding business things when I am supposed to be on vacation. I also appreciate how Ashley does wellness checks of our community and network. I believe my prayers have been answered regarding my team. Because of them, I can focus on growing the business and grow as a leader. If your team is not holding you accountable for your goals, then you all need to do some internal checks and ask yourself what you are doing it all for. A team should not only support you on your entrepreneurial journey, but it should also help grow you. Accountability is the best way to do just that.

Teamwork is Crucial to Your Success
Lastly, I will say that being in this Empowered Sisters Network mastermind has allowed me to grow tremendously, mainly because I am surrounded by like-minded women who truly want to see each other win. It is truly an honor to be connected to these powerhouses. When I first had the idea of starting the mastermind, my goal was to have a group for accountability. I had set bodacious goals for myself in my business and life and was struggling to accomplish some of them, so I wanted to meet with a few ladies that I trusted and for us to hold each

other accountable regarding our goals. It was great and accomplished exactly what it was intended to do. But this new iteration of the mastermind is the brainchild of Ashley Knight. She has grown this mastermind into a true sisterhood of successful, bold women going after big goals in their businesses and lives. The student has become the teacher, and I am here for it! I am honored to be a part of this amazing group. My final piece of advice to you is to build a strong team and find a mastermind to join. Entrepreneurship is not for the faint of heart, but you can make it with a strong team supporting you.

Breakout Questions

How did you get started in business?

_____

_____

_____

_____

_____

_____

_____

_____

_____

_____

_____

_____

_____

_____

How are you doing in business now?

_____

_____

_____

_____

_____

_____

_____

_____

_____

_____

_____

_____

_____

Grandpa

~Ashley Marie~

MY GRANDPA TAUGHT ME SO MANY LESSONS. My grandma (on my father's side) taught me so many more things. You see, I never lived in the same state as both of my grandparents in my entire life being influenced by them, but they both had such great impacts on my life.

They never let me feel alone. Even when they were so far away, I always knew they loved me, and they were there for me. They wrote me letters for as long as I can remember and that followed me up through my adult life. When I went into the military in locations like Iraq, Germany, and Hawaii they always found a way to get me a letter in the mail. I have always appreciated them both for that. Why did I share this with you? Well, this to me exhibited that you don't have to be in someone's presence to leave an impact. As a person exhibiting an infectious Boss Character, your presence should linger beyond your being in the room. My grandparents never had to be in the same state as me to influence love and consideration in my heart. It calls for effort when you are trying to impact intentional relationships. As a Boss in this century, you may influence your community in many ways via virtual space or in person, but you should still be able to be approachable and respected. This experience from my grandparents taught me to go the extra mile. It taught me to consider others. I am sure you know that life moves at a million miles a minute.

Breakout Question

Let's Go Forward~Take your chances and go for it.
Since it is a fact that in this present state:
You can't go back
You can't stay here
Let's Go Forward

Using the statement: "What the heck, go for it anyway!"
Make a list of 10 aspirations that you would like to accomplish.

_____

_____

_____

_____

_____

_____

_____

_____

_____

_____

_____

_____

Follow up all 10 aspirations with 3 steps that will help you reach these goals. (If you don't know how get in the room and ask an expert who can help you learn how.)

_____

_____

_____

_____

_____

_____

_____

_____

_____

_____

_____

Execute them one at a time, closing them out as complete in the next 12 months.

Go beyond the doubts!

Blessed are the poor in spirit for theirs is the kingdom of heaven.
Matthew 5:3 KJV

Chapter 5

The Challenge

I AM NOT ONE THAT SITS around watching TV all day, but I do believe it was in this location, in front of a television set, that my husband asked me to watch a show that changed me in a mighty good way from that point on.

If you haven't seen it, I am going to ask you to take some time to watch the Undercover Billionaire challenge with Glenn Stern. It was in this moment of leisure activity that I asked my husband to pause the show because I had to run and get my notebook.

I was literally surviving on big event after big event or sales spike after sales spike as a small business owner. There is no real relief unless you can truly master the flow of sales. As I began to watch this show I was blown away about how outside of the box this challenge was with a goal to create a business worth 1 million dollars. I jotted down so many notes as to how I could earn money daily, network with the community around me, and use the resources within my community better. The biggest note I wrote down was how I could make 1 million dollars. Now if you truly calculate it, you have earned and brought in over 1 million dollars in your time in the workforce. The question lies in the "How do I maintain and retain this funding?" That is when I got the crazy idea to bring this idea to my small group of professionals and asked them the question. "Who would like to be a millionaire in 12 months with me?" Everyone of course was like I would but how??? As I detailed to them about the show and how it inspired me to try this with our group, I got so many mixed feelings and responses.

At the end of that task, I invested in 11 ladies with $100 each to start this Undercover Billionaire Challenge as a group. The guidelines were that we as a group would operate as one unit to earn 1 million dollars in 12 months. We were moving and shaking and within
three months of this journey we had already had over $90,000 in contracts and over $15,000 in cash between all accounts. We began to see the finish line and we have been on this journey ever since.

Breakout Session

How you do anything is a matter of commitment. How committed are you to reaching your goals?

_____

_____

_____

_____

_____

_____

_____

_____

_____

_____

_____

_____

How much effort or investment do you put into reaching your goals?

_____

_____

_____

_____

_____

_____

_____

_____

_____

_____

_____

_____

_____

_____

Most importantly, who are the individuals who are helping you achieve those goals?

_____

_____

_____

_____

_____

_____

_____

_____

_____

_____

_____

As a bonus, we encourage you to watch the TV show '*Undercover Billionaire*' challenge that features the journeys of Grant Cardone, Monique Mosley, and Elaine Culotti on Paramount+.

Climb Higher

Go Deeper

Reach Farther

Dream Bigger
Thou therefore endure hardness, as a good soldier of Jesus Christ.
II Timothy 2:3

Chapter 6

Let Go to Go On

~Larisha Perlote~

A Divine Strategy

AS I CONTINUE TO REFLECT on what the word BOSS means to me and what is required to be a BOSS, I cannot help but to think of Joshua and the Israelites amid the battle of Jericho. To paraphrase, in the book of Joshua we find the Israelites led by Joshua (the successor of Moses) who conquered the heavily fortified city of Jericho. The battle strategy employed holds profound significance in the use of military tactics and faith. The city of Jericho is well-known for its impenetrable walls. Joshua, given a divine strategy, commanded his army to march around Jericho once a day for six days with seven priests carrying trumpets made of ram's horn. (The seventh day would prove to be an epic victory). The priests led the procession which created an atmosphere of anticipation as well as curiosity among the inhabitants of Jericho. You can say this constant encirclement raised questions about the Israelites intentions and posed some psychological pressure on the city's defenders. Joshua had to be a BOSS to move as God called him. We see boldness, movement in an official capacity, strategy, and singleness of heart within the plan for his life (and those attached to him).

A Dream

I believe one of the many ways God speaks to His children is through our dreams. If we are not attentive to His voice, we can miss His instruction. (Stay with me, I promise you I am going somewhere with this.) In August 2006, I experienced a permanent change of station to Shaw Air Force Base, South Carolina in preparation for my next deployment in the United States Army. This reassignment and subsequent deployment would geographically separate me from my husband, my daughter, my newborn son (~3 months at the time), my church family, friends, and everything I found ***comfort in.*** While this was not my first deployment, it would prove to be a profound wilderness experience. Have you ever encountered your own "wilderness experience"? Ponder this, the U.S. National Parks Service defines wilderness in this manner: areas that offer solitude through remoteness and primitive and unconfined recreation by cutting out influence from mechanized forms of interaction. (Did you get that?!) In other words, I separated from everything that was familiar, safe, comfortable, and convenient to walk into ***a part*** of the plan for my life.

In September 2006, during my evening bible study, I read Ezekiel, chapters 3, 4, and 33 which focused on a minister's duty. Additionally, I was reading Matthew 28:17-19 and fell asleep shortly thereafter (Do not judge me.). I dreamt I was walking on a wooden pier or a plank-like structure. I intentionally and delicately walked to the edge of the pier, stopped, and peered into the water postured all around. The smell of the water resembled salted seawater; it was familiar. As I peered into the water, I saw a ship in the distance moving in the opposite direction. As I continued to peer into the water, I realized I was naked except for an item fastened to my butt (Stay with me, I promise I am going somewhere!). I managed to remove the item but could not make out what it said. I believed it to be a scripture, a warning, or instructions. In the blink of an eye, there was a shift in the dream; I went from the pier to an unfamiliar house. Just as quickly as the setting changed, I received a phone call from my husband, and he instructed me to *"GO QUICK."* I woke up shortly thereafter and prayed for clarity, or an interpretation, but received nothing until a week before my deployment overseas.

A Deployment

In October 2006, I deployed to a designated location in the Army Central Command's Area of Responsibility. While my unit executed a complex, coordinated, combat mission; my role was simple: manage a small team trained to collect, analyze, and prepare data for senior command decision-makers. My role required accuracy, timeliness, and relevance of information collected by my team. These abilities involved coordination with related units and personnel, overseeing data collection processes, and maintaining the integrity of the data throughout its analysis and preparation phases. This role required an elevated level of attention to detail, as small errors in the analysis could have significant consequences for mission planning, execution, and most importantly impact the lives of the innocent and our service members. I know, you may be asking why is she saying all of this and what is the relevance to BOSS Character. ***Ponder this:*** My ability to effectively communicate the findings of the analysis to senior military leaders was crucial for informing strategic decisions and adjusting tactics as needed in response to the changing circumstances in the air and on the ground. Not clear enough? I employed boldness, operated in an official capacity, moved strategically and with singleness of heart to complete the mission. I was called to BOSS up!

A Distraction

Truth be told, with any mission, task, or anything we are called to do – we have choices. We can apply our God-given, God-driven skills, abilities, and attributes OR allow them to lie dormant and unused. We cannot afford to ***sit*** on what has been gifted to us. I encourage you, my sister, and my brother – get up! I want you to know that with every mission, task, or anything we are called to do there will be periods or points of distraction. In my wilderness experience, I encountered postpartum depression, separation anxiety, and dealt with sexist and discriminatory unit leadership during my deployment. Wait Larisha, you said postpartum depression?

Yes, I said postpartum depression. You see, I was called to a permanent change of station while pregnant with my second child. I reported to the new Army unit ~3 months after I had my son. I waited an additional month (doctor-directed) and waived the Army's full postpartum recovery period to deploy with the new unit (my choice because I was already geographically separated from my husband, daughter, and infant son). I know, how crazy is this? What sensible mother would leave her nursing infant? What sensible person would leave their place of comfort and peace for war? Remember, I shared that we have choices – my choice albeit painful and detrimental at the time proved to catapult my life (and my family) to a destination beyond what we could have asked, thought, or imagined. My sister and brother, "All things work for the good." Our choices, points of distraction, and even the pain are all a part of God's divine plan or strategy for our lives.

The Destination

Dr. Myles Monroe, stated, *"God will show you your vision, but never tell you how you are going to get there, and there is a reason, because your vision is a glimpse of your end. Between the end and where you are is called the plan. The plan is the process that takes you to your destination."* Dr. Monroe explained Joseph's dreams, specifically when Pharaoh placed him in charge of the land of Egypt, only second to Pharaoh (see Genesis 41:30-44). Dr. Monroe shares, *"God will tell you your end, just like He showed Joseph on the throne, sitting on the throne ruling, feeding his brothers, that is the end. God showed you your end. He showed each one of you your end, but He never tells you the plan. Why? Because if He ever told you the plan you will tell Him forget the destination. **Because the plan is to prepare you for the destination**; He takes you through all these different changes to **develop you.** If Joseph knew he had to go to a pit and prison to get to the throne, he would tell God forget the throne. Right now, where you are may not be where you want to be, but it is a part of the plan…God is working on character development, patience development, vision development. **He is preparing you for what He prepared for you.**"* You see, you are not where you are by chance, happenstance, or luck, there is a divine strategy for your life. My sister, my brother, everyone attached to you (yes you!) will prosper as you walk out this plan, this divine strategy. Know that you are not reading this book, this chapter, this page, this sentence for nothing. This moment is a part of the plan, ***the divine strategy for your life***.

Listen, I cannot leave you hanging regarding the interpretation of the dream. Remember, I was walking intentionally and delicately on the wooden pier or plank-like structure? Well, the ***walking*** is reflective of my ***personal journey with God and his preordained plan for my life***. The water (salted) represented the Word of God all around me (and in me – after all I am "the salt of the earth." (Matthew 5:13).) Understand this, salt draws out the good flavor subtly hidden in a thing and preserves it so it will not spoil! (Did you catch that? That will preach!). Peering into the water, realizing my nakedness and the item fastened to my butt reflected vulnerability, yielding, and served as a warning. You see, I was sitting on the God-given gift and if I did not ***GO QUICK***, I would miss the boat (hence the ship in the distance moving in the opposite direction). I later awoke with a quickening in my spirit to read Matthew 28:17-20. It reads, "And Jesus came and spake unto them, saying, all power is given unto me in heaven and in earth. Go ye therefore, and teach all nations, baptizing them in the Name of the Father, and of the Son, and of the Holy Ghost: Teaching them to observe all things whatsoever I have commanded you: and, lo, I am with you always even unto the end of the world. Amen."

You have what it takes to get there! We just get comfortable in life...

~Ashley Knight~

Breakout Session

How do you handle your distractions?

_____

_____

_____

_____

_____

_____

_____

_____

_____

_____

_____

_____

_____

_____

What are your common distractions?

_____

_____

_____

_____

_____

_____

_____

_____

_____

_____

_____

_____

Block out the noise!

Get focused in order to clearly hear, see, and execute.

Chapter 7

Unity

~Felisha Gibson~

Product Producing BOSS

I STARTED DIVINE WORKS GLOBAL LLC so that it would expand to a fruitful platform for my legacy. It all started with someone asking about how I grow my hair. As an adult, along with being in the military, I noticed that my hair would only grow about shoulder length. Though as a child my hair would grow to about to the middle of my back or longer. After looking at old photos of myself I had the desire to try to grow my hair again. It had been about 30 years since I'd seen my hair that long. So, I started researching things I could do to encourage hair growth.

God has given us everything on this earth to sustain us. In my research I found that:

Thick hair requires:
*apple cider vinegar
*coconut oil
*avocado oil
*peppermint oil
*aloe vera

Thin hair needs less oil. In my research, I found that apple cider vinegar and aloe vera could help strengthen hair. Apple cider vinegar can also improve the luster of the hair to include helping with itchy scalp. Olive oil is most beneficial for dry, thick hair. Coconut oil is used to relieve dandruff and restore luster and protect the hair. Avocado oil can help nourish the hair and scalp. Lastly, I found that peppermint oil carries traits that promote hair growth as well. From all this information collected, I started applying these items to my hair while wearing protective styles and my hair started to grow again. It was stronger and healthier than I had ever seen. I had a lot of shedding before I started using the oils. From there, the shedding decreased, and it also helped with itching and dandruff. Once I started putting my hair in protective styles for about 3 months at a time, I noticed my hair was growing and healthy, so I continued to use the oil and I kept my hair on a 3-month protective style schedule. This progress inspired me to start Divine Work Natural Hair Oil production.

I had a few of my friends try it out to see if it worked for them. They had great results using the products as well. To elevate things a little further one of my friends Marsha invited me to a mastermind meeting that happens weekly. She sent me the link. I listened in on the call and found these amazing, awesome women working together to help one another in their individual business goals. These ladies were where I wanted to be. Here I was just starting my business, coming up with a name creating the LLC, opening business accounts, applying for grants, and the rest is history. Being around people who were making forward moving actions excited me. These are things that most of them had already been doing and had achieved. I felt that in this room, I could do it too.

Reflecting on my military career and relating to some of these ladies in the group and their military service, I was blessed not to see a deployment unlike some of the other ladies in my 10 years, 2 months, 18 days in the military. But I did have field exercise and training that took a toll on my hair, not to mention the stress that comes with the job. My hair was thick and started to become thin and it was constantly breaking off, so it no longer retained length. I started cutting it thinking if I kept it trimmed it would start to grow back and it didn't. It would get to a certain length and stop for years. The oils became my remedy to get back to a full and healthy head of hair. It then became a producer of revenue for me. To see a little girl go from little growth to a noticeable growth in 6 months was amazing. To have customers come back and purchase more because they could see the results on the product was even more exciting. I have seen this oil help people with alopecia and people going through cancer treatment with hair loss.

Managing my finances|
In 2014, God showed me a plan to get out of debt. My husband was stationed overseas, and my first-born child was going off to college at the age of 16. So, here

100

we are in three different locations around the world. My son in Georgia, my husband in Germany, and me and my other three kids in Texas. All of us needed a place to stay, food to eat, and a way to get around. So, money was tight, and we had to make it go a long way. The first thing God showed me was that we needed a budget. It needed to be written down. Absolutely everything that needed to be paid, this included all our expenses, i.e.: gas, food, and clothes. We needed to make sure that every dollar had a home. Once I was able to see how much money was being spent versus how much was coming in, I made the necessary adjustments to work for each household. It took us four and a half years to get out of debt. By Jan 2019 we were out of credit card debt, then in May 2022 we paid our last house note payment. This freed us financially to save for retirement and vacations. It also put me in a confident space to feel comfortable to start my business in financial coaching and natural hair oil. As I looked around, I could see people struggling to make ends meet, living paycheck to paycheck. I wanted to teach them how God taught me to get out of that same position, so I came up with a monthly planning and goal tracking sheet. When you see where your money is going, it makes it easier to put a plan together to achieve those goals and make everything work for you and your family.

Getting ahead and making your money work for you can eliminate the stressors that come with life when you have financial concerns. With this sheet each family had to make a plan that works for them. So, my budget may have looked a little different because of my priorities and the needs of my family versus the needs of yours. Look on the following pages to view a copy of the Divine Works Finance & Budgeting Worksheets.

The ultimate goal is to make sure that our needs are taken care of versus our wants. This is the most manageable way for you to get out of debt and live in a wealthy state of peace and freedom in your finances. I believe these practices aligned me with this group that helped me grow my money as well as gave me the right headspace to create a product that I can sell.

Monthly Bill Estimate

$

Salary	Amount
Primay Check	$
2nd Check	$
3rd Check	$
4th Check	$
5th Check	$
6th Check	$

Income Monthly Total $

Name of Bills	Amount Due	Amount paid	Remaining
Tithes and offering	$	$	$
Emergency saving	$	$	$
House Repair savings	$	$	$
Car Maintenance saving	$	$	$
Christmas/ Birthday saving	$	$	$
inventments/ Roth	$	$	$
Montagage/ Rent	$	$	$
Car Payment	$	$	$
Car Insurance	$	$	$
Health Insurance	$	$	$
Electric bill	$	$	$
Water bill	$	$	$
cat/dog food	$	$	$
Credit Card	$	$	$
Credit Card 2	$	$	$
Credit Card 3	$	$	$
Credit Card 4	$	$	$
Credit Card 5	$	$	$
Hair and Nails	$	$	$
Groceries	$	$	$
Eating out fund	$	$	$
Gas	$	$	$
Clothes	$	$	$
petty Cash/ Unexpected expenses	$	$	$
Total	$	$	$

Monthly Bills

Account	Beginning Balance	Amount Added	End of the Month
Tithes and Offerings	$	$	$
Monthly Account for Needs	$	$	$
Monthly Bill Account Only	$	$	$
Savings Account (IE Car or Trips)	$	$	$
Emergency Account $2500.00	$	$	$
Total Cost	$	$	$

2024

	Monthly income
Weekly Check	$
Weekly Check	$
Weekly Check	$
Weekly Check	$
Weekly Check	$
Weekly Check	$
Total Income	$

Car saving	$		
Christmas saving	$		
Trip saving	$	$	$
Electric Bill	$		
water bill	$		
USAA Ins	$		
Home owner's ins	$		
Time Warner Cable	$		
Vivint	$	$	$
AT&T Wireless	$		
Credit card	$		
	$		
	$		
	$		
	$		
Tithes and offering	$	$	$
Petty cash	$		
Gas	$		
Savings	$		
Food	$	$	$
Total Cost	$	$	$

103

Monthly Bill Planner

Pay Period _____

	Jan	Feb	Mar	Apr	May	Jun	Jul	Aug	Sept	Oct	Nov	Dec

Pay Period _____

	Jan	Feb	Mar	Apr	May	Jun	Jul	Aug	Sept	Oct	Nov	Dec

Clarity comes from engagement…

~Ashley Stahl~

When you are going through tough times...
Good habits aren't enough to keep you on track.

~Amy Morin~

Every Small change is worth the effort... Take the Step!

~Ashley Knight~

Breakout Activity

Producer Mindset over Consumer Mindset

Are you a producer or are you a consumer? It's okay for you to be both but to what capacity are you engaged in both? Let's break it down.

_____

_____

_____

_____

_____

Producer Mindset
Invest, invest, invest.
Sell, sell, sell.
Create, create, create.

Consumer Mindset
Buy, buy, buy.
Purchase, purchase, purchase.
Use, use, use.

Grant Cardone said, *"A wealthier life requires multiple streams of income."*
Never depend on one flow of income. Here are some examples of revenue streams:
    -Trust
    -Investments
    -Government Contracting
    -Wealth/Savings/Inheritance
    -Wealth Walk/Wealth Talk
    -Entrepreneurship
    -Work promotions/salary increases

Take the leap of faith and believe that everything is going to be alright.
If you trust yourself, it will come to you right when you need it.

"Stop complaining and produce!"

~Les Brown~

Breakout Question

How much research have you put into the work you desire to conduct?

_____

_____

_____

_____

_____

_____

_____

_____

_____

_____

_____

_____

Have you concluded that you are your first business client?

_____

_____

_____

_____

_____

_____

_____

_____

_____

_____

_____

_____

Breakout Question

What is debt stopping you from accomplishing?

_____

_____

_____

_____

_____

_____

_____

_____

_____

_____

_____

_____

_____

Have you created a plan to manage your finances?

_____

_____

_____

_____

_____

_____

_____

_____

_____

_____

_____

_____

_____

What mindset are you carrying? Are you a Producer or a Consumer?

_____

_____

_____

_____

_____

_____

_____

_____

_____

_____

_____

_____

_____

_____

Believe

Chapter 8

Check your Pulse - Temperance is LOVE'S victory.

~Ashley Marie~

WHEN THE HEAT IS ON, HOW DO YOU PERFORM?

At the slightest disruption of your plans do you get frustrated, delusional, and hard to get along with? Are you calm, controlled, and present in the moment? Does fight or flight kick in, readying your feet to jump into action? How does your heartbeat? The key to being a tolerated and revered boss is to be able to truly "Watch thyself!" Control under fire is required on any given day as a leader of a diverse population. What style of temperament do you exhibit? Most surveys of any staff population when asked will rate their Boss as one who is either a good Boss or a bad Boss.

These surveys may conclude that the staff deems their Boss as a good Boss who exhibits these characteristics:

Good Boss
Shows empathy
Listens
Present in the moment
Considerate
Approachable

Bad Boss
Arrogant
Unapproachable

Inconsiderate
Disconnected

Just to name a few. When it comes to being a Boss the key here is to remember that *trouble doesn't last always, this too shall pass* in any given situation. The way you operate and speak in your area of influence will shift the atmosphere that you aim to impact. Aim to stay in the positive lane and don't let the issues that arrive weigh you down. Leading any population requires a leader that always stands on sturdy ground. Others can be influenced to do their best in environments that communicate consistently. Others know when your heart is in something or out of something. Others naturally match the effort and energy that is displayed by their leaders. Infect others to believe in the overall mission. Stand strong in your mission and move beyond the challenges quickly. There is nothing more damning than an environment that cannot move beyond the offenses. The focus in any unified effort must be to keep progress flowing forward.

It boils down to a heart thing. Scripture states in Matthew 12:34, *Out of the abundance of the heart the mouth speaks*. Whatever you harbor in your heart, your mind will think, and your mouth will speak. Ensure that you are conducting regular heart checks on yourself and those that you influence. Just as you go to the doctors regularly to ensure that your body is healthy and whole, you must section off time to check the hearts of those that you impact.
These simple questions can assist that the hearts of your team are stable.
Ask:
How are you doing?

Gesture:
Do you congratulate your team on wins that are achieved together?

_____

_____

_____

_____

_____

_____

_____

_____

_____

_____

_____

Relate:

Do you make a point to meet, at least weekly, to connect with and get to know those that you are leading?

_____

_____

_____

_____

_____

_____

_____

_____

_____

_____

Sometimes we get in the way of our future and our success. Just remember these things

~Check the heart daily.

~Move out of the way.

~Don't limit GOD!

~Realize how privileged we are in Christ. His hands are bigger than ours.

~We have a direct connection to the resources needed to accomplish our heart's purpose. All we must do is **believe**.

None of us are immune from crisis.

~Ryan Holiday~

Revived into Position

~Taunya Ford~

IN A WORLD OF MULTIPLE PERSPECTIVES and definitions of terms like BOSS and BEAUTY, I aspire to stand as a shining example of a servant leader and an effective communicator in my community. So, before I start this journey on revived boss beauty, I will begin by providing a reference for a few terms before we buckle up for this ride.

What is my perspective of the common term BOSS? This is going to be fun. I will use an empowering acronym when reflecting on the term BOSS–Bravely Overcoming with Sisterhood Strength. By sharing my journey, I hope to be a testament to the revived beauty and power of sisterhood where circles of women are recognized for assisting me when my cup ran empty by reviving my determination, compassion, and the relentless pursuit of self-discovery.

As I embarked on this mission, my heart held onto a profound belief:
~ I could finally define or understand my revived beauty.
~The essence of my beauty goes above what others define of me as beauty.
~ This goes beyond a physical realm of beauty.

It would be small pockets of friendship circles that would show me a revived meaning of beauty. As I felt my new revived beauty resided deep within my soul, I was patiently waiting to be discovered, nurtured, and revived for myself, by myself. My pain with beauty was now being empowered by others; it was now about having the audacity to confront my vulnerabilities, embrace my imperfections, and harness the inner strength required to overcome life's formidable challenges. These challenges, often referred to as disabilities by society, included my diagnosis of lupus and alopecia, along with my journey through post-traumatic stress and epilepsy.

During my suffering and struggles, I discovered that my path to 'BOSS Revived Beauty' need not be a solitary one. The multiple medical conditions that once made me feel invisible, overlooked, rejected, and isolated could, in fact, be blessings in disguise. I found solace and purpose in connecting with support groups, where I realized that my pain was not just my pain. I learned of others hurting, suffering, and wanting to survive in the same situation. I now focused past my pain, to how my pain could pave the way to support others and create a supportive sisterhood. These newfound communities, filled with like-minded women and even a few supportive men, became pillars of strength during times when my strength became unsteady.

Through my relentless pursuit of self-improvement, I encountered numerous moments of doubt, adversity, pain, and insecurity. Little did I know, these were the cocoon moments of my revived beauty transformation. Just like a profound metamorphosis a caterpillar undergoes with the shedding of its old form to emerge as a beautiful butterfly, I needed to shed my old insecurities, fears, and doubts. I did so by not only finding my inner strength but also by seeking support from a community that genuinely cared about my well-being.

During these challenging times, I unearthed the extraordinary power of self-belief intertwined with the unwavering support of sisterhood and extended family. Over 25 years, individuals from various chapters of my life–be it high school, college, or comrades from my military service–stood by my side. They unknowingly became pillars of inspiration, offering their strength and encouragement, oblivious to my silent battles with depression. Their words and actions were a lifeline, propelling me through my darkest moments. Their presence is a beacon of hope, illuminating my path with love. Amidst my struggles, a multitude of women of unwavering strength were silently fostering empowerment and encouragement within me. I emerged from my cocoon, an even more resilient and beautiful version of myself.

For so long, I held the role of the unyielding pillar of strength for others, yet in doing so, I neglected the fragility of my spirit. My unwavering commitment to aiding and guiding others had become second nature, while the vulnerability of seeking help for myself remained uncharted territory. It was a humbling realization that amidst my ability to guide and protect others, I faltered in extending the same compassion and care toward my well-being. In this journey of self-discovery and healing, I learned that vulnerability is not a sign of weakness but rather a testament to courage and authenticity. It is through acknowledging my limitations and reaching out for support that I discovered the true strength in vulnerability. With the unwavering support of my sisterhood and extended family, I embarked on a transformative journey towards self-compassion and self-discovery.

Today, in this new chapter, I am filled with gratitude for the profound impact of sisterhood, formal and informal, and the power of self-belief. Through their love, encouragement, and unwavering support, I have emerged from the depths of despair and transformed into a beacon of resilience and beauty. As I continue to navigate life's challenges, I do so with the newfound wisdom that true strength lies not in trying to do everything alone, but in embracing vulnerability and seeking support from those who stand ready to uplift and empower me. The loss of my career due to medical diagnoses of lupus and chronic post-traumatic stress had me questioning everything about my purpose and my beauty. I found myself adrift, feeling lost and unseen, and without a sense of purpose. But my journey to "BOSS Revived Beauty" mirrored the transformation of a caterpillar into a butterfly. It necessitated shutting down my insecurities, facing my fears and doubts head-on, and relying on the strength of support groups and sisterhood. It was a spiritual revival, a rebirth of my true self, and the rekindling of my spirit with a renewed sense of purpose.

In my previous life as an Army signal officer, I had a clear understanding of my purpose. However, retirement ushered me into a world where I felt lost, and my self-worth questioned by medical conditions that affected my physical appearance. Amidst stress, depression, anxiety, and the loss of my hair, I struggled to see myself as beautiful in a world that often equates beauty with the physical attribute of hair.

Yet, the turning point arrived when I chose to focus on self-care and self-prioritization. I had been selected for a second chance, and I would now treat myself with the same level of care and importance I routinely extended to others. I realized that while I saw the importance of someone making me a priority, I hadn't made myself one.

Retirement from the military, a blessing in itself, left me broken and confused for five years. My desire to prevent others from experiencing the same feelings drove me to give of myself endlessly, often neglecting my responsibilities and well-being. I signed up to be everyone else's cheerleader but had stopped showing up for myself.

My turning point came when I found myself teetering on the brink of ending my life, engulfed by despair and hopelessness. It was a dark time, fraught with overwhelming challenges—from grappling with the complexities of lupus and epilepsy to waging a relentless battle against chronic depression, loneliness, and anxiety. In the depths of my anguish, I reached out to a higher power, pleading for the revival of my beauty and a glimmer of purpose amidst the excruciating pain that engulfed me. I was uncertain what form this revival would take. I held onto a flicker of hope amidst the darkness that threatened to consume me.

Then, in late December of 2021, something shifted within me after struggling with chronic depression and the feeling of being bullied amidst my suicidal thoughts. I fell to my knees and called on God and asked Him how I was supposed to help people when I received no help for myself. Afterward, I called several friends and discussed living with a vision and a mission, then I created my yearly vision board that helped me refocus my life, reminiscent of my military days. I finally saw the possibility of finding purpose within my pain.

My journey to "Revived Beauty" stands as a testament to the power of **B**ravely **O**vercoming with **S**isterhood **S**trength. It's a journey that continues to unfold. A journey of resilience, self-discovery, and transformation that I share with the world. I hope to inspire others to embark on their own paths toward rediscovering their unique revived beauty and strength. This is just a snapshot of my "Revived Beauty BOSS" story. It stands as a testament to the spirit of a female Veteran. We are warriors and survivors.

Together, let us embark on this incredible journey of self-discovery, empowerment, and growth. Life's challenges may seem overwhelming when faced alone, but when we tackle them together, they transform into opportunities for unity, support, and shared experiences. On this path, we can uncover the truest forms of our beauty, and even on the toughest days, we can uplift and inspire one another.

On this journey called life, challenges are inevitable, but so are triumphs. Some chapters will find us as fans, students, or teachers. There will be times when life celebrates us, then there will be times when life tests us. Throughout the journey, we emerge with powerful stories of successes and struggles that could have broken us but didn't, thanks to the strength of our sisterhood.

Through my experiences, I have grown and revived my beauty not only physically but emotionally, intellectually, and spiritually. These scriptures offer valuable insights into the concepts of revival and beauty, both from a spiritual and emotional perspective. They have served as a source of inspiration and guidance on my journey toward understanding and embodying 'Revived Beauty'. May you also find strength, purpose, and inspiration in your exploration of these biblical snippets that I will share.

Scriptures referencing 'Revived'.

Genesis 45:27 - *And they told him all the words of Joseph, which he had said unto them, and when he saw the wagons which Joseph had sent to carry him, the spirit of Jacob their father revived.* KJV

Psalm 85:6 - *Wilt thou not revive us again, that thy people may rejoice in thee?* KJV

Isaiah 57:15 - *For thus saith the high and lofty One that inhabited eternity, whose name is Holy; I dwell in the high and holy place, with him also that is of a contrite and humble spirit, to revive the spirit of the humble, and to revive the heart of the contrite ones.* KJV

Habakkuk 3:2 - *O Lord, I have heard thy speech, and was afraid: O Lord, revive thy work in the midst of the years, in the midst of the years make known; in wrath remember mercy.* KJV

Isaiah 38:16 - *O Lord, by these things men live, and in all these things is the life of my spirit: so wilt thou recover me, and make me to live.* KJV

Scriptures referencing 'Beauty'.

2 Chronicles 20:21 - *And when he had consulted with the people, he appointed singers unto the Lord, and that should praise the beauty of holiness, as they went out before the army, and to say, Praise the Lord; for his mercy endureth forever.* KJV

Psalm 27:4 - *One thing have I desired of the Lord, that will I seek after; that I may dwell in the house of the Lord all the days of my life, to behold the beauty of the Lord, and to inquire in his temple.* KJV

Psalm 50:2 - *Out of Zion, the perfection of beauty, God hath shined.* KJV

Isaiah 52:7 - *How beautiful upon the mountains are the feet of him that bringeth good tidings, that publisheth peace; that bringeth good tidings of good, that published salvation; that saith unto Zion, Thy God reigneth!* KJV

Song of Solomon 4:7 - *Thou art all fair, my love; there is no spot in thee.* KJV

These verses indeed offer profound wisdom and inspiration for those seeking spiritual and emotional renewal, as well as a deeper appreciation of beauty in various forms. May these scriptures continue to be a source of strength, purpose, and inspiration for you and for all who embark on their own journeys of self-discovery and transformation. May we all find the beauty and revival that resides within us and in the world around us.

Like a caterpillar's transformation into a butterfly, I've learned to shed my past self and embrace every step of my metamorphosis. My journey reflects my unwavering commitment to growth, evolution, and becoming more than I ever imagined. And it's all possible with the incredible support of my diverse sisterhood and circle of friends.

Change is an inevitable part of life, and I've learned to fully embrace it. I've become adept at navigating life's unexpected twists and turns, finding resilience and transformation at every corner. Just like a butterfly spreading its wings, I've embraced change, seeing the world and myself in a new light while understanding my purpose with greater clarity.

From the depths of my roller coaster life experiences, I've drawn strength akin to that of a lioness. Despite facing challenges such as suicidal ideation, depression, PTSD, epilepsy, lupus, alopecia, MST, surviving sexual assault, and the emotional impact of a hysterectomy, I've emerged stronger, with a brand-new attitude.

Today, I am thrilled to reintroduce myself as "Revived Beauty BOSS" because it was through trials and contemplating suicide that I found my rebirth. In my darkest moments, when I called out to God for hope and asked Him to Revive my

BEAUTY, He showed me my village—the family and friend angels that have always been by my side, and He added to my village, sending me on a new mission.

In my sanctuary, I've transformed pain into purpose by continuing to support others who have supported me and by extending that support to women like me surviving medical hair loss. I offer a private but personal understanding and a safe space to navigate their journeys. However, this journey wouldn't be possible without persistence, transformation, strength, and the openness to rediscover ourselves.

These pillars have been instrumental on my "Boss" journey, embodying bravery and resilience, the transformative power of growth, and the strength to face adversity. As "Revived Beauty BOSS," I embrace these qualities wholeheartedly, knowing that they have shaped me into the empowered individual I am today, ready to inspire and uplift others on their paths of rediscovery and transformation. Our stories transcend mere trials; they are narratives of emergence and transformation. We are more than our illnesses, our diagnosis, our successes, and our challenges; we are warriors and survivors. Let's celebrate this incredible journey together, embracing ourselves each day with the strength of sisterhood. Through diversity, we find unity and strength. It is within our circle of trust that I discovered unwavering encouragement, and it was within many circles that I found the purpose of my pain.

Sisterhood is not just about receiving support; it's about empowering each other. It's about giving support and encouraging one another to embrace vulnerability, confront fears, and embark on paths of personal growth. Together, we can shatter the glass ceilings of social expectations and find strength in unity. The power of sisterhood lies in our collective strength, and, like a tapestry woven from different threads, we are held together by our shared experiences, perspectives, and stories. Together, we create a rich and vibrant narrative, a beautiful tapestry of resilience and transformation.

So, let us remember that true strength is not done existing alone but amplified when shared with others. We are here to empower one another, celebrate each other's uniqueness, and find purpose in our collective journey. Together, we are unstoppable, and together, we show that there can be purpose in pain. Revived

Beauty became my new mission, a sanctuary where pain transformed into purpose, supporting women with diagnosed medical hair loss. It offered them a haven of understanding and a private space for those walking similar paths. But this journey required persistence, transformation, strength, and openness to rediscovery. These pillars define my continuous Boss journey, embodying the essence of bravely overcoming.

Our stories are more than trials; they are narratives of emergence and transformation, a journey from caterpillar to butterfly and lioness. It encapsulates growth, change, service, strength, compassion, and the spirit of warrior survivors. Let's celebrate this transformative journey together, embracing ourselves with sisterhood strength.

I'm fortunate to be surrounded by an incredible sisterhood of all colors, shapes, and sizes—a diverse network of individuals offering strength, compassion, and understanding. Together, we've pushed boundaries, providing unwavering support. Within this circle of trust, I found encouragement to continue my journey without surrendering to life's challenges.

True strength isn't solitary; it's amplified when shared. In this compassionate and understanding sisterhood, I have discovered the true essence of beauty—the beauty of genuine human connection. Through support, encouragement, and love, I've undergone a soulful metamorphosis.

As I celebrate my journey as a Revived Beauty BOSS, I extend my heartfelt gratitude to my sisters, both near and far, you know who you are. We may not share the same mother, but you have been my pillars of support, proving that beauty isn't defined by social standards but by the strength, resilience, and love we share.

Transformation and empowerment are at the core of our journey, just like the butterfly emerging from its cocoon. We are ready to set flight and inspire others. Our collective strength propels us forward, breaking barriers, shattering stereotypes, and rediscovering the very essence of beauty.

My Boss journey is a testament to the power of bravery, sisterhood strength, and transformation. It's a journey of growth, empowerment, and embracing change.

I invite everyone to join us in celebrating resilience and beauty. Stand at the crossroads of our collective experiences and embrace your Boss, your Revived Beauty. As we rise and take our place at our respective crossroads of our collective experiences, I extend an invitation to you to embark on your own BOSS journey. Whether you are a survivor like me, who has moved from suffering to surviving with, diagnosed medical hair loss, a veteran undergoing a different transformation, or someone dealing with life's challenges, know that you are not alone, and know that you are already beautiful. There is a village or a sisterhood waiting for you, and there is strength within you to find and join a team that will be better for having you.

Here are some steps that helped me embark on a BOSS journey:

1. Seek Support: Reach out to support networks, whether through organizations, peer groups, empowering networks, military affiliates, cultural organizations, religious support groups, or your local communities' organizations. Seek the companionship and guidance of those who have walked a similar path or seek those that are walking a path that you want to walk.

2. Celebrate Your Beauty: Remember that you define your beauty, and that beauty resides within you every day. Celebrate your beauty, the way you see it, and not the way that society depicts beauty because your beauty has uniqueness, your beauty has strength, and your journey towards self-discovery and empowerment is beautiful.

3. Find Your Strength: Explore your inner strength. Don't run from the greatness that you can become because you're worried that somebody else will see it. When you find your strength, you will also be able to recognize your resilience and courage. Recognize that you possess the power to overcome adversity and emerge stronger.

4. Build communities, Sisterhoods, or Brotherhoods: Foster diverse connections with individuals who positively challenge you, uplift, and inspire you. Surround yourself with a circle of support that understands and celebrates your journey even when you are not in the same room.

5. Embrace Change: Recognize that to embrace change you don't have to agree with it or support it, but when we recognize that embracing change can be a beautiful part of life, we're most likely to become a butterfly because we change from the caterpillar after being in a cocoon. Yet through that change, we see something that is equally beautiful, and we welcome that change is a part of life,

and transformation is a powerful force for growth. Embrace the ups and downs that come with change as an opportunity to become a better version of yourself.

6. Empower Others: As you embark on your BOSS journey, acknowledge that you are already beautiful and pay it forward because somebody needs you. Empower others who may be struggling without forgetting your own beauty, offering them the support and strength they need to thrive but do not put your beauty on the back burner.

7. Share Your Story: This one was hard for me, and I work on it every day, but I tell you with confidence that you need to share your story because it has the potential to inspire others. Share your experiences, both positive and negative, but it's OK for you to also recognize your triumphs, and challenges to create a ripple effect of empowerment.

My BOSS journey to Revived Beauty has been a roller coaster journey that I almost quit multiple times, even to the extent that I would've not been able to come back from, but my journey has also been one of growth, newfound understanding, purpose, transformation, and village growth and strength. I hope that this narrative not only inspires and empowers individuals, but it also motivates them to embrace their journeys with revived beauty.

Together, let us continue to revive and redefine beauty, celebrate our inner strength, and aspire to inspire a world where everyone can embark on their own BOSS revived beauty journey of transformation and empowerment.

There is beauty in the journey so stay the course because My BOSS Journey Continues. As we continue our exploration of the BOSS journey to Revived Beauty, we will continue to dig deeper into the transformative power one can find within resilience and the impact of embracing one's unique path.

Resilience: In the heart of every BOSS journey lies the remarkable quality of resilience. It is the ability to bounce back from difficulty and to withstand life's challenges while emerging even stronger. Resilience is a piece of the puzzle that brings the other pieces together with the needed pieces of our stories, and it is through the challenges we face that we will discover our strength and our capacity for growth.

In my BOSS, Revived Beauty, journey, resilience displayed itself to me in countless forms. It was the strength to overcome the physical and emotional toll of the medical conditions that had control over me. It was the courage to personally confront the scars of my military service that I ignored with my successes, and the shadows of depression that almost killed me. It was the determination to rise above the bullying that happened to me and the suicidal thoughts, that I emerged as a guiding light of hope and inspiration.

As I look back on my path to Revived Beauty that saved my life, I see resilience as the bridge between my former self and the empowered revived individual I am becoming today. It is the BOSS Revived Beauty that has allowed me to shed the limitations of my old self, just as a butterfly leaves behind its cocoon. Resilience and a village of diverse supporters were the transformative energy that propelled me towards embracing my BOSS journey with a new unwavering determination.

Embracing the Unique Path: One of the most beautiful aspects of a Revived Beauty BOSS journey is its unique and personal nature when you have a diverse supportive team. No two journeys are or will be identical, for each of our paths is shaped by our experiences, challenges, and aspirations. Embracing this uniqueness is a celebration of individuality and the recognition that our diverse travels contribute to our rich tapestry of life.

Throughout my BOSS journey, I learned to value the beauty of connections and of my struggles, and the beauty in pain and success. I realized that my path, with all its roller-coaster twists and turns, was a testament to my resilience and strength. It reflected my willingness to confront adversity head-on and to emerge with newfound wisdom and grace.

Every person's journey to Revived Beauty is a unique story waiting to be told when you're ready and how you are ready to share it. It may be beauty marked by medical challenges, personal transformations, or the pursuit of inner peace and self-acceptance. Regardless of the path, what unites us as BOSSES is our commitment to embracing our journey with the support of our empowered networks, maintaining principles of understanding, love, diversity and inclusion, selfless service, and allowing our stories to be shared when we're ready because it takes a real BOSS that has revived their beauty to be comfortable in sharing our stories and empowering others to do the same.

Breakout Testimony

Cast Out Doubt

When you lose all hope…cast out doubt. Find someone stronger than you in that moment so that you won't quit on yourself.

I wrote this letter believing that I had no other choice but to pull out of the race and give up on something I desperately needed.

Dear Ashley,

I am reaching out with a heart full of mixed emotions to inform you of my decision to withdraw from the current BOSS challenge. This decision, influenced by recent lupus flare-ups, last-minute travels, and new responsibilities has led me to this step that I take with both pain and optimism. Prioritizing my new responsibilities is crucial, especially under these challenging circumstances.

At the heart of my commitment, launching my business demands my undivided financial dedication. My mission to support those with medical hair loss is more than a business—it's a calling. This commitment has become even more pressing as I take on the role of medical proxy for my sister, who is battling schizophrenia and recently underwent the amputation of fingers. My care responsibilities for her have understandably intensified.

Given these factors, fully engaging in the BOSS challenge is currently beyond my capacity. However, I am deeply interested in joining Phase 2 of your program. The value of mentorship and growth it offers is something I earnestly look forward to, along with the opportunity to bring three women with me to share in this enriching experience.

As I navigate through this period, the spirit and lessons of your program remain close to my heart. As I attend various women's conferences promoting Revived Beauty LLC, I will be sharing ESN collective stories. Moreover, the recent addition of a business partner for the next 24 months marks an exciting turn in my professional journey.

On a personal front, I am planning a move to Las Vegas within the next year, signifying a new chapter in both my personal and professional life. With this move, I am exploring the possibility of converting my current home into a rental or Airbnb.

Your understanding and support during this time means the world to me, Ashley. Your mentorship has been lifesaving and a source of inspiration and strength, and I am eager to reengage with your program in Phase 2, when the time aligns.
You are a BOSS inspiration. Thank you.

Thank you for this circle of women on this journey.

Sisterly Love
Taunya

Things to remember to stay on course:
- Keep your hearts and minds aligned.
- Stay focused.
- Take refuge in Him.
- Choose your focus. Choose it wisely. Make choices that you can live with.
- Our reality is determined by where we direct our eyes ~Camryn Dudley~
- Allow God to move undeniably in your life. You don't know what you don't know. Don't fall out before you gain the manifestation of the seeds you plant. Allow the fruit to bloom.
- Always remember–God has preloaded you with what you need before you know you need it. (GOD IS LOVE)

~Kriskeya Price~

The Ups and Downs During the Challenge

I was invited to a challenge that commenced in October 2023, sparking my initial excitement. I saw this as a great opportunity to save more and deepen my understanding of money. Ashley initiated the challenge by providing each participant with $100 to open a checking account. Finding an account offering a specific amount upon opening proved challenging, but I eventually located a suitable bank in Temple, Texas.

Initially, I leveraged my gifts and talents to earn money for the challenge. However, when January 2024 arrived, panic set in. I mistakenly believed each participant had to individually accumulate a million dollars by October 2024. Drawing inspiration from the Undercover Billionaire TV show, where real estate played a crucial role, I decided to explore ways to achieve this staggering goal. Curious about the daily earnings needed, I turned to Google and discovered it would require around $2740 a day—a daunting realization considering my modest monthly deposits. Frustrated, I sought guidance and arranged a meeting with Dr. Ann after receiving an email invitation. During our discussion, I anxiously inquired about others' progress, desperately asking if there were real estate deals that could expedite my earnings. Dr. Ann calmly explained that the challenge was collaborative, with the collective goal being to reach a million dollars. Taking a deep breath, I recognized the varied strategies the other participants were employing—selling clothes, capitalizing on business ideas, and even finding joy in small amounts like coins. I resolved to move forward, continuing to utilize my gifts and talents to build my challenge accounts. Despite the fluctuations, this journey is teaching me valuable lessons and helping me save money in various aspects of my life.

To stay focused, I turned to Proverbs 3:5-6 *Trust in the LORD with all your heart, and do not lean on your own understanding. In all your ways acknowledge him, and he will make straight your paths.* I encourage everyone to formulate a plan, set a budget, and embark on their financial challenge. I believe in my ability to become a millionaire one day–with God, all things are possible.

Things to come...
Would you consider participating in a challenge like this one?
One where the goals are beyond sight and understanding?

Breakout Activity

What is your life's assignment?

_____

_____

_____

_____

_____

_____

_____

_____

_____

_____

_____

_____

_____

How did you come to gain this assessment?

_____

_____

_____

_____

_____

_____

_____

_____

_____

_____

Time and time again my influence on the life of others has rendered great results either financially or mentally. I know I am gifted at igniting the fires in others. I don't allow life's distractions to derail me from my assignment. Over the years, as I have grown to have a closer walk with my Lord and Savior Jesus Christ, I know He has my back. He has shown me repeatedly how He does what He promises He will do. All it requires of me is to stay in the positive lane and to have a character of peace, love, and longsuffering.

~Ashley Marie~

*I am a beacon of light that infects success on all
that I come in connection with.*

~Ashley Marie~

Special entry from additional participants of the challenge

What made you decide to take control of your money position?

The reason I decided to take control of my money position is because I was tired of living paycheck to paycheck. I was tired of constantly wondering whether or not I would have the right amount of money to make purchases to provide for my family's needs while trying to manage three different households at one time.

~ Felisha Gibson ~

I took control of my finances when my daughter was diagnosed as having special needs. I never wanted my mistakes with money to ever impact her future. She was and still is my why! Over the past year, I realized that I've gotten content. Yes, I'm in a blessed position but it could be better. I decided I needed to stop maintaining but to multiply!

~ Dr. Ann James ~

I decided to take more control of my money position because I always played it safe. There was little to no risk which were missed opportunities. I just need to take the leap of faith and do something different.

~Larisha Perlote~

I feel as if I've been pushed into a pause in life and I am really disliking it. I realized I partnered with poverty and needed to change things. The Undercover Billionaire Challenge showed me it is possible. I need this to manifest primarily for ME.

~Marsha Martin~

I realized I had become comfortable with my finances because all the bills were being paid, I was able to save, and I was able to run my business. Then life took a turn that disrupted my comfort. I don't like being uncomfortable, especially with my finances. This change was necessary so that when life throws curveballs, I'm not thrown off my financial plan and goals for my family.

~Lila Holley~

How big is your why?

My why is to show my kids they don't have to depend on a 9-5 job. God has gifted all of us with talents that we can use to be successful if we take the time to develop the skills God has given to us.

~ Felisha Gibson ~

My why is bigger than me. It's about the generations after me. My family has moved in "not enough or just enough". We have forgotten...or maybe never seen the fullness of what God has for us. It's time to walk in that fullness (in every area of life).

~Larisha Perlote~

My why is generational. I am now sowing into my daughter, nieces, nephews, and grandchildren. I want to be able to leave an inheritance to my family. Not only leave an inheritance but teach them how to better manage their money and grow their wealth.

~Lila Holley~

ABOUT THE AUTHORS

The Visionary-Ashley Marie

Ashley Marie aka Mrs. Positivity lives in the positive lane. She focuses on influencing those around her in a positive way in hopes of helping others to present their best selves.

She is an international best-selling author "Women on a Mission" and a bestselling author "Behind the Rank Vol 1 and Vol 4. She has published over 9 books. Ashley is a serial entrepreneur. Ashley is a wife, mother and positive life influencer.

Sayings: "Do Better When You Know Better" "Never settle for less than the best"

Co-Author Lila Holley

Lila Holley is a multi-award-winning, bestselling author, Army Veteran, and founder of Camouflaged Sisters. She uses her books and real-life lessons to help other Service Members maneuver through the emotional battlefield of transitioning from the military, take ownership of their stories, and heal using the power of storytelling. The Camouflaged Sisters anthology series consists of 9 published books sharing stories from 143 courageous military women. The books cover topics such as leadership, mentorship, sisterhood, career challenges, and combat experiences. They also tackle tough topics like surviving military sexual assault, toxic leadership, PTSD, and surviving domestic violence while serving. These authors desire that other women read their stories and know that they are not alone in their struggles. This method of writing and storytelling is healing for both the writers and the readers. Lila believes there is no one better to tell these stories than the women who lived them. Learn more at camouflagedsisters.org.

"Being a part of this mastermind has been incredible. I've grown so much as an entrepreneur. I think the greatest part of this journey is being able to glean from these amazing women."

Co-Author Larisha Perlote

Larisha Perlote is a wife, mother, grandmother, Army Combat Veteran, licensed marriage and family therapist, and entrepreneur. She is the owner and Clinical Director of Heal(ed) for the Journey Counseling & Consulting, LLC in Texas.

At *Heal(ed)* for the Journey; she *educes* (draws out) problematic ways of thinking and being, *edifies* (builds up) those that are broken-hearted, and *educates* (teaches) individuals, couples, and families on how to overcome relational abandonment, abuse, rejection, and trauma. Larisha facilitates collective growth, healing, and wholeness through authentic, compassionate, faith-based, therapeutic, and psychoeducational services.

Larisha believes people want to be healed, however they just don't know how. Join her in an "unraveling" session and choose to heal!

Co-Author Felisha Gibson

In 2023, Felisha embarked on a transformative journey by founding Divine Works Global LLC. Passionate about empowering women, she established a natural hair oil business under the company's umbrella. Felisha's mission is to enlighten women on the power of nurturing their hair with natural elements bestowed upon us by God, fostering the growth of strong and healthy hair.

Going beyond hair care, Felisha extends her impact by offering personalized financial coaching services; she is dedicated to guiding individuals towards financial success. With a commitment to breaking the cycle of living paycheck to paycheck, Felisha's one-on-one coaching sessions aim to empower people on their journey to financial well-being.

Through Divine Works Global LLC, Felisha not only celebrates the beauty of natural hair, but also strives to uplift individuals by providing the tools and knowledge needed to achieve financial freedom. Her dual focus on both natural beauty and financial empowerment reflects a holistic approach to enhancing lives.

Co-Author Charmella Daniels

Charmella Daniels is a business owner and entrepreneur. She is a natural leader and uses her experiences and expertise to teach, mentor, and coach others. Her niche is assisting new & start-up companies understand business principles from the beginning.

Her educational background consists of a BS in Business Administration with a concentration in supply chain management. She is a professional commercial driver and has over 22 years of logistical experience.

Charmella is a wife, mother of 3 sons (2 of them Sailors) and 4 grandchildren. She is also an Army Combat Veteran who continues to serve her community.

Co-Author Taunya Ford

US Army Major (Ret) Taunya Latausha Ford's journey through life has taken her from the picturesque snowcapped mountains and landscapes of Colorado Springs, Colorado, to the desert heat and bustling city of Las Vegas, Nevada, where she pursued her education and graduated from the University of Nevada Las Vegas and received her Army commissioned as a Field Artillery officer in the United States Army.

Co-Author Brandy Davidson

Brandy Davidson is an Army Veteran, bestselling author, mother, and friend. She is the owner of Purposed Project Management Services where she relieves other business owners and CEOs of stress, by serving as an event coordinator, project manager, or administrative executive.

The vision for Purposed Project Management Services is to help other business owners lead their companies strategically and build a winning team.

"If you want to go fast, go alone. If you want to go far, go together."
-African Proverb

Brandy believes that smiling can change someone's day without saying a word.

List of books that were read during this challenge.

1. *Stillness is the Key* by Ryan Holiday
2. *Profit First* by Mike Michalowicz
3. *15 Secrets Successful People Know About Time Management: The Productivity Habits of 7 Billionaires, 13 Olympic Athletes, 29 Straight-A Students, and 239 Entrepreneurs* by Kevin Kruse
4. *I Will Teach You to Be Rich* by Ramit Sethi
5. *The Mountain Is You: Transforming Self-Sabotage into Self-Mastery* by Brianna Wiest
6. *The Story of Three Little Divas Reach Your Money Goals in 3 Steps Before You Huff and Puff Your Next Paycheck Away* by Brandy Baxter
7. *10X Rule* by Grant Cardone
8. *Find Your Why* by Simon Sinek